The answer is only a simple DNA test away. In this charming book, photographer Grace Chon pairs stunning portraits of mixed-breed pups with their DNA breakdowns, revealing the origins of their adorable quirks—from long bodies and stubby legs to that one floppy ear that refuses to stand up straight. Sometimes funny, sometimes surprising, and always exceptionally lovable, *What Kind of Dog Is That?* is a must-have for every dog lover.

What Kind of
Dog Is That?

What Kind of Dog Is That?

Loveable Mutts & Their DNA Results

GRACE CHON

Foreword by Dr. David Haworth, Embark Veterinary

Countryman Press

An Imprint of W. W. Norton & Company
Independent Publishers Since 1923

To Vin, Jasper, and Elliot

Printed in Vietnam
First Edition

For information about special discounts for bulk purchases, please contact W. W. Norton Special Sales specialsales@wwnorton.com or 800-233-4830

Manufacturing through Asia Pacific Offset

Countryman Press
www.countrymanpress.com

An imprint of W. W. Norton & Company, Inc.
500 Fifth Avenue, New York, NY 10110
www.wwnorton.com

978-1-68268-964-6

1 2 3 4 5 6 7 8 9 0

CONTENTS

FOREWORD

All dogs are beautiful. I say that as a person who has dedicated his life to caring for these creatures. They are special thanks to their spirit, the close bond they share with us, and the roles they play in our lives, families, and communities. Dogs not only enrich our world with love, companionship, and joy; they also bring us humans closer together. Walking up to a stranger on the street is awkward until dogs are in the picture, which changes everything. And what's the most common first question? "What kind of dog is that?"

Photographer Grace Chon's portraits of mixed-breed dogs—mutts—give readers a chance to really study characteristics that can give us hints to a dog's heritage. But when she teams up with advances in science, using DNA kits from the pioneering company Embark Veterinary, the picture really comes into focus. After all, how do we define what makes the dogs in our lives so uniquely . . . them? It's in their DNA. The basic genetic code, made up of billions of combinations of the same four molecules that determine every living thing on this planet, also makes each of these dogs one of a kind.

Embark Veterinary was founded on the science behind finding the answer to that question. Our cofounders—two brothers who are also scientists and dog lovers—set off across the globe to get DNA samples from every kind of dog. They tested village dogs and community dogs from Iceland to Papua New Guinea, from Siberia to Patagonia. That data has been life-changing, and helped build a base of knowledge that keeps growing.

Our dogs' genes play an important role in their physical appearance, their health, their behaviors, and even influence how perceptive their noses can be. By magnifying certain traits over generations, humans created specialist dogs in all sorts of areas. Great Danes are guard dogs; they are usually not great at long-distance running, but are really good at making sure homes remain protected. All breeds with "Retriever" in their names—Goldens, Labradors, Chesapeake Bay—were bred to do exactly that, retrieve. Most Retrievers stay true to that behavior by happily fetching any objects thrown by their owners. There are even breeds designed specifically to be ideal companions, like the Maltese, an ancient breed known to be charming, friendly, and attentive. DNA is a window into what makes the hundreds of dog breeds that surround us as diverse as they are.

Scientists already know a lot about dogs and their DNA, but in many ways, we are just at the beginning of our understanding. Like the first pages of an extraordinary book, our knowledge of all the ways genes interact together keeps inviting us to find out more. The dogs highlighted in this book are stunning in their diversity, each one as unique as their genetic makeup.

Guessing a dog's breed mix from their appearance is a popular game, and one we invite you to play along with throughout this book. Though a dog may look like one breed, their DNA often tells another story. Embark Veterinary customers tell us that uncovering these surprises with their dog brings them closer together, and can improve the ways in which they care for them.

DNA can even help dogs find their forever homes. The shelters and animal rescue organizations we partner with tell us that DNA testing helps them inform potential adopters about all aspects of their new family member before bringing a dog home. A more informed adoptive family means a better fit and a better chance of a forever match. Veterinarians and their staff use genetic testing to assess and understand known health risks, which can inform their clinical recommendations and potentially prolong or improve a patient's quality of life by monitoring their health and catching issues before they become serious.

We're glad to join Grace in celebrating the beauty of dogs by helping us all understand this key component of their makeup—the very DNA of their lives.

DAVID HAWORTH, DVM, PHD
Executive Vice President, Research & Development
Embark Veterinary

INTRODUCTION

I've been a dog photographer for 17 years, and the question I get asked the most is, "What's your favorite dog breed?" And though there are hundreds of recognized dog breeds around the world that I could choose from, I've always had the same response: "My favorite dog breed is a mutt!"

Mutts are 100 percent unique, and when I see a mutt, I see a limited edition work of art. As soon as I meet one, in seconds I've already taken inventory of all the things I find endearing and uniquely adorable about the dog. Is it their long body and stubby legs? Is it their one floppy ear that refuses to stand up straight? Is it the complete mystery of what dog breeds could have possibly contributed to this mash-up of cuteness?

I'm continually astounded by the mind-blowing diversity of dogs, and the magic that happens when multiple breeds come together. Dogs actually share more than 99 percent of their DNA with wolves, but thanks to natural and artificial selection through breeding, that 1 percent difference has created the vast diversity we see in dogs. In other words, only 1 percent of a dog's genes determines the wide range of physical appearance, size, and shape we see. According to research from Stanford University, dogs are the physically most diverse land animal, thanks to years of breeding for specific purposes and traits. Now dogs can be small enough to fit in a purse, and large enough to stand taller than a human. You couldn't blame an alien visiting Earth for the first time if they thought that a Chihuahua and a Mastiff were two completely different species!

Mutts truly show off nature's infinite creativity in the most fun and unexpected ways.

But trying to take a crack at guessing their ancestry can be challenging. Veterinarians, shelters, and rescue groups can only make their best guess based on appearance. But because there is so much variation in dogs' looks, determining the breed of a dog by looks alone is an unreliable method.

This is where genetic testing comes into play. As dogs have increasingly become family members in households around the world, interest in dog DNA tests have surged. These tests are especially popular among people who have rescue dogs with an unknown background. According to the Associated Press, more than a million dogs have been DNA tested in a little over a decade. And with millions of dogs adopted during the COVID-19 pandemic, many owners have been left wondering about their dog's ancestral lineage.

Thanks to advances in science that have made DNA testing easier and more accessible, there's a much better chance of figuring out what dog breeds make up our unique mutts and their one-of-a-kind package of cute.

Each dog photographed for this book has been tested with one of the most accurate dog DNA tests in the industry by Embark Veterinary, a global leader in dog health and genetics. This allows you to learn what mix of awesomeness went into creating every adorable feature of each pup. And if you find yourself wondering what a "supermutt" is, it's a dog whose ancestry includes traces of many different breeds, each contributing just a tiny fragment of DNA. The DNA segments are so small that they can no longer be clearly assigned to a specific breed. The results are sometimes funny, sometimes surprising, but always beautiful and exceptionally adorable.

This book is a celebration of these marvelous mutts that we all love and are so curious about. My hope is that you experience delight over each limited edition, furry masterpiece as much as I have. And now, thanks to Embark Veterinary, we can finally have some answers to the question, "What kind of dog is that?"

THE Dogs

Daisy

13 YEARS

47.5% Chihuahua
39.9% Cocker Spaniel
12.6% Bichon Frise

Gives free high fives to everyone who wants one, and is always ready to spread some cheer.

Duncan

5 YEARS

49.6%	American Pit Bull Terrier
14.1%	American Staffordshire Terrier
11.2%	Poodle (Small)
7.0%	Bulldog
4.9%	German Shepherd Dog
13.2%	Supermutt

Has webbed feet and joyfully retrieves floating Frisbees from rivers, lakes, and oceans to his heart's content.

Ruthie

3 YEARS

27.1% Chihuahua
24.1% Shetland Sheepdog
22.4% American Pit Bull Terrier
12.7% Boxer
13.7% Supermutt

Makes biscuits with her paws like a cat when she's sleepy.

Teddy

12 YEARS

92% American Staffordshire Terrier
3% American Bulldog
3% Neapolitan Mastiff
2% American Pit Bull Terrier

Loves to insistently yell at his family when he wants something, especially food or a walk.

Kendi

5 YEARS

33.4% Dogue de Bordeaux
32.6% Siberian Husky
19.7% German Shepherd Dog
11.1% Chow Chow
3.2% Supermutt

Squeezes his big body into the smallest, most uncomfortable looking spaces to sleep.

Jack

7 YEARS

42.0% Poodle (Small)
28.3% Bichon Frise
17.1% Rat Terrier
12.6% Chihuahua

Grabs his favorite toy and runs around with it in his mouth when his favorite people come over.

Harrison

4 YEARS

48.1%	Chihuahua
10.7%	Russell Terrier
9.2%	Pomeranian
9.0%	Pekingese
8.1%	Poodle (Small)
5.5%	Dachshund
9.4%	Supermutt

Adores being stuck to his mom's side like Velcro and is the absolute sweetest, most cuddly pup you'll ever meet.

Pua

5 YEARS

46.2%	Basset Hound
30.3%	Siberian Husky
10.2%	Alaskan Malamute
5.4%	German Shepherd Dog
4.1%	Akita
3.8%	Golden Retriever

Loves to lie down in the center of the yard and contemplate deep, philosophical ideas first thing in the morning.

Juniper

3 YEARS

30.1%	Chihuahua
22.1%	Poodle (Small)
14.5%	Cocker Spaniel
7.1%	Maltese
7.0%	Pomeranian
6.9%	Dachshund
4.0%	Miniature Pinscher
8.3%	Supermutt

Destroys any and all toys when given the opportunity.

Harley

4 YEARS

38.5% Chihuahua
20.4% Poodle (Small)
6.8% Pomeranian
6.1% American Eskimo Dog
4.6% Pekingese
4.5% Bichon Frise
19.1% Supermutt

Turns into a gremlin after 9 PM and bites your feet when it's bedtime.

Gomez

1 YEAR

84.7% Japanese Chin
15.3% Pekingese

Goes completely limp during cuddles, melting into your arms as if all his bones just disappear.

Enzo

5 MONTHS

57.0%	Yorkshire Terrier
16.8%	Poodle (Small)
5.9%	Shih Tzu
20.3%	Supermutt

Waits for his family to get home so he can steal their socks and shake them around like a toy.

Clive

3 YEARS

31.0% Poodle (Small)
21.7% Chihuahua
13.3% Rat Terrier
9.0% American Eskimo Dog
7.7% Pekingese
6.9% Pomeranian
10.4% Supermutt

Has human eyes and looks at people intently as if he's about to speak (or maybe give a TED Talk).

Candy

14 YEARS

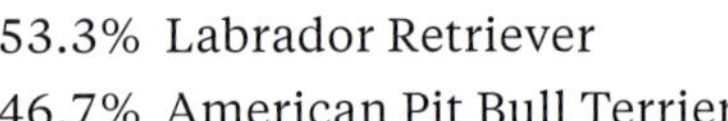

53.3% Labrador Retriever
46.7% American Pit Bull Terrier

Loves one-on-one snuggle time on a blanket outside in the grass—especially when it involves nail trims.

Celine Dion

2 YEARS OLD

34.7% German Shepherd Dog
24.4% Australian Cattle Dog
12.3% Golden Retriever
8.1% Weimaraner
6.3% Rottweiler
14.2% Supermutt

Tenderly looks after her pet rock, carrying it everywhere she goes and playfully pouncing on it when it's time for fun.

Mookie

3 YEARS

18.5% Chihuahua
17.5% German Shepherd Dog
15.7% Poodle (Small)
14.5% American Pit Bull Terrier
13.6% Australian Cattle Dog
20.2% Supermutt

Greets everyone like a long-lost friend, and loves to snack on large leaves of romaine lettuce.

Sticky

3 YEARS

54.7% American Pit Bull Terrier
18.1% Chihuahua
7.8% Rat Terrier
19.4% Supermutt

Stretches out across the back of the couch with her legs sticking straight up in the air, usually snoozing away with a toy tucked between her paws.

Johnny

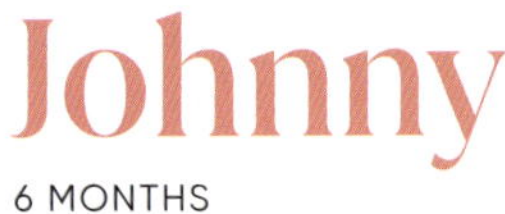

6 MONTHS

42.9%	Siberian Husky
12.7%	Cocker Spaniel
11.7%	German Shepherd Dog
4.5%	Yorkshire Terrier
28.2%	Supermutt

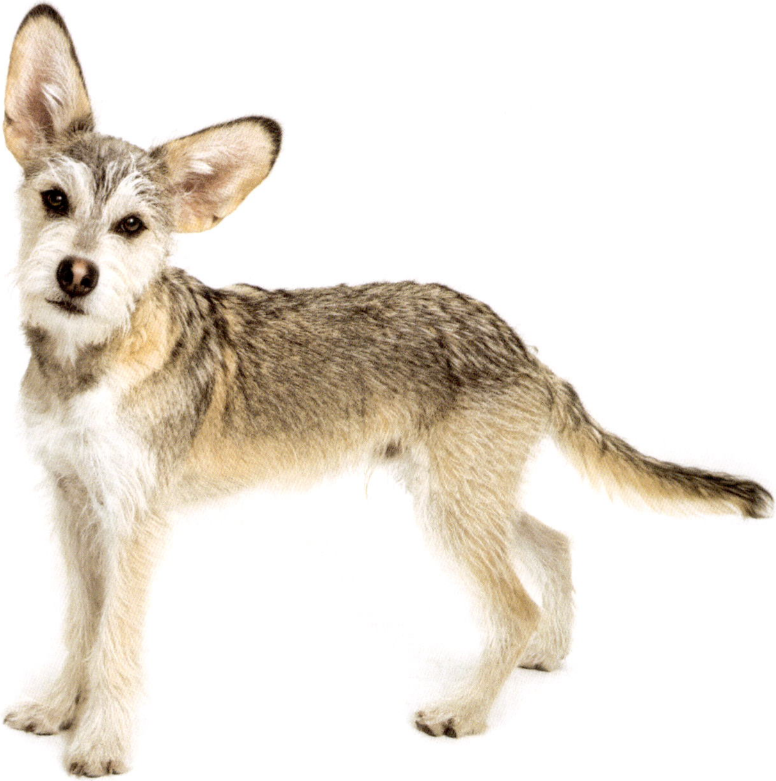

Steals his family's underwear and jumps like a mischievous kangaroo.

Chloe

10 YEARS

16.8% Beagle
14.5% Australian Cattle Dog
13.2% Chow Chow
10.7% Boxer
8.0% Siberian Husky
7.3% Cocker Spaniel
6.8% Shiba Inu
22.7% Supermutt

Grunts with pleasure when she gets pets and scratches, and likes to herd her mom and dad around the house.

11 YEARS

31.1% Chihuahua
26.2% Poodle (Small)
21.2% Rat Terrier
10.8% Shih Tzu
5.7% Miniature Pinscher
5.0% Pekingese

Rolls around on her back and barks with glee after a good meal—but only if she thinks no one is watching!

Pip

8 WEEKS

27.7% Miniature Pinscher
24.2% Chihuahua
11.8% Pug
11.0% Poodle (Small)
5.8% Maltese
4.5% Pekingese
15.0% Supermutt

Believes he's the biggest dog in the pack even though he's 50 pounds less than the next smallest pup in the family.

Bailey

3 YEARS

83.2% American Bully
8.3% Poodle (Small)
8.5% Supermutt

Hops onto a chair, leans back, and sits right beside you at dinner like a distinguished gentleman, just to be part of the conversation.

Hero

10 YEARS

53.3% Chihuahua
18.0% Rat Terrier
7.9% Bichon Frise
7.6% Maltese
4.9% Poodle (Small)
4.5% Miniature Pinscher
3.8% Pekingese

Transforms from being a shy introvert to smiling with her entire body when the lights and camera are on her.

Frankie

3 YEARS

30.0% Siberian Husky
19.6% American Pit Bull Terrier
11.1% Chow Chow
8.7% Belgian Malinois
8.3% German Shepherd Dog
8.2% Cocker Spaniel
14.1% Supermutt

Enjoys chasing birds, staring contests (she aways wins), and splooting the day away.

Madison

13 YEARS

50.0% Yorkshire Terrier
25.6% Shih Tzu
24.4% Pomeranian

Enjoys playing dress-up and picking out her own outfits like a little canine fashionista.

Nova

4 YEARS

37.2% Australian Cattle Dog
19.8% Labrador Retriever
17.0% American Pit Bull Terrier
12.3% German Shepherd Dog
6.5% Border Collie
7.2% Supermutt

Wildly smart and learns new things as soon as you show her.

Chance

3 YEARS

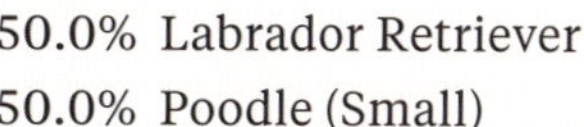

50.0% Labrador Retriever
50.0% Poodle (Small)

Gives great hugs, with legs like human arms that can wrap completely around people.

Buddy

17 YEARS

78.3% Pomeranian
7.4% Shih Tzu
14.3% Supermutt

Hard of hearing but an incredible listener, and maintains eye contact like no other.

Wookie

5 MONTHS

59.8% Shih Tzu
24.3% Labrador Retriever
15.9% Pekingese

Endlessly curious and is friends with a squad of furry and feathery friends—cats, chickens, and even a baby pig.

Yeti

15 YEARS

31.2% Poodle (Small)
27.4% Siberian Husky
11.1% Chow Chow
4.6% Shetland Sheepdog
4.5% Pekingese
3.7% Shih Tzu
17.5% Supermutt

Looks at you as if she's just about to say something . . . and then burps like a human.

Popeye

11 YEARS

21.5% Shih Tzu
18.7% Poodle (Small)
17.3% Pomeranian
15.5% Maltese
14.6% Chihuahua
12.4% Rat Terrier

Known as Popeye the Foodie, but is actually the world's pickiest eater.

Beta

10 YEARS

23.7% American Pit Bull Terrier
20.1% German Shepherd Dog
18.7% Chow Chow
6.7% Collie
30.8% Supermutt

Loves the great outdoors and is fiercely independent, but always roams close enough to watch her family from a distance.

Nova

6 YEARS

37.9% Miniature Pinscher
14.7% American Bully
14.3% Chihuahua
7.8% Golden Retriever
6.6% Maltese
5.5% Pekingese
13.2% Supermutt

Likes to chomp talk: snapping her teeth together like an enthusiastic snapping turtle, all without making a sound.

Miles

5 YEARS

53.8% Chihuahua
26.1% American Bully
11.1% Pekingese
9.0% Shih Tzu

Finds his happy place watching episodes of The Nanny—
Fran Drescher's voice makes his tail wag.

Milo

1 YEAR

28.5% Chihuahua
24.5% Poodle (Small)
16.2% Yorkshire Terrier
7.6% Cocker Spaniel
7.1% Pekingese
4.9% Pomeranian
11.2% Supermutt

Hugs people like he's a friendly toddler—the mail carrier, Amazon delivery drivers, Postmates couriers, everyone.

Moo Goo

1 YEAR

51.9% Australian Cattle Dog
23.6% American Pit Bull Terrier
11.2% German Shepherd Dog
13.3% Supermutt

Has attended house parties, a comedy club, an acting course, and a few short film shoots.

Yoda

5 YEARS

66.1% Chihuahua
11.4% Poodle (Small)
9.5% Shih Tzu
5.7% Pomeranian
4.3% Maltese
3.0% Yorkshire Terrier

Delights in people humming near her cheek and even tries to hum back in response.

Elliot

3 YEARS

50.0% Siberian Husky
22.5% Chihuahua
9.8% Poodle (Small)
8.3% Yorkshire Terrier
5.7% American Staffordshire Terrier
3.7% German Shepherd Dog

Highly intelligent, cerebral, and always eager to share his opinions with anyone willing to listen.

Ellie

3 YEARS

49.4% Yorkshire Terrier
45.2% Miniature Schnauzer
5.4% Standard Schnauzer

Loves warm-hearted souls, and greets them with a happy dance on her hind legs.

Max

4 YEARS

47.2% Poodle (Small)
28.1% Chihuahua
8.6% American Eskimo Dog
5.0% Pekingese
4.7% Bichon Frise
6.4% Supermutt

Snuggles into bed and rests his head on a pillow, just like a human.

Fauna

1 YEAR

26.4% Chihuahua
16.5% Poodle (Small)
14.0% Rat Terrier
9.6% Pug
6.7% Miniature Pinscher
5.9% Dachshund
3.7% Maltese
17.2% Supermutt

Watches TV as if she understands it all.

Moe

8 YEARS

35.6% Poodle (Small)
34.2% American Pit Bull Terrier
16.9% American Staffordshire Terrier
13.3% Supermutt

Gives kisses on both cheeks, like he's French.

Peanut

6 YEARS

40.5% German Shepherd Dog
22.8% American Pit Bull Terrier
13.3% Chow Chow
13.2% Rottweiler
10.2% American Staffordshire Terrier

Catches treats thrown at her with expert timing on the count of one, two, three!

Pony Danza

13 YEARS

27.1% American Pit Bull Terrier
26.4% American Bully
26.1% Dalmatian
20.4% Chihuahua

Jumps on the garage roof to sunbathe and survey the neighborhood, to the delight of all the neighbors.

Masha

7 YEARS

31.9% Poodle (Small)
21.5% Chihuahua
12.0% Shih Tzu
8.2% Cocker Spaniel
6.5% Shetland Sheepdog
5.3% Pug
14.6% Supermutt

Perches on her mom's shoulder like a bird and enjoys going for walks—she's part acrobat, part parrot.

Odie

4 YEARS

18.5% Boxer
15.4% Golden Retriever
9.9% Pomeranian
8.9% Poodle (Small)
8.7% American Pit Bull Terrier
8.0% Cocker Spaniel
7.4% Labrador Retriever
23.2% Supermutt

Doesn't feel the need to people please, so when he chooses you for cuddling it's very, very special.

Lola

12 YEARS

36.7% Chihuahua
19.2% Shih Tzu
17.1% American Eskimo Dog
8.7% Poodle (Small)
8.0% Cocker Spaniel
10.3% Supermutt

Loves to push electronic devices away for extra cuddle time and undivided attention.

Rio

8 YEARS

81.2% German Shepherd Dog
17.3% Siberian Husky
1.5% Supermutt

Prefers to sleep on the cold floor and uses his dog bed for enjoying his favorite treats.

Squid

15 YEARS

50.0% Poodle (Small)
30.0% American Bully
13.1% American Pit Bull Terrier
6.9% Neapolitan Mastiff

Crosses his front paws like a polite gentleman when he's lying down.

Hiro

8 YEARS

32.2% Chihuahua
28.6% Shih Tzu
9.3% Poodle (Small)
8.8% Pomeranian
7.0% Miniature Pinscher
6.4% Dachshund
7.7% Supermutt

Loves to get pampered and have his hair combed with a toothbrush.

Millie

11 YEARS

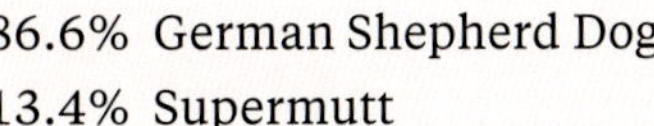

86.6% German Shepherd Dog
13.4% Supermutt

Stomps her feet to be let outside and clinks the food or water bowl with her paw when she wants it filled.

Barney

11 YEARS

29.9% American Pit Bull Terrier
19.3% Basset Hound
13.2% Beagle
9.6% Golden Retriever
28.0% Supermutt

Takes walks to places where he knows they give away treats.

Joey

6 YEARS

59.5% Chihuahua
7.6% Poodle (Small)
6.2% Cocker Spaniel
6.1% Pomeranian
20.6% Supermutt

Just wants to be loved and cuddled 24/7, and has almost no other interests in life.

Vegeta

1 YEAR

45.9% American Pit Bull Terrier
33.8% Siberian Husky
14.2% German Shepherd Dog
6.1% American Bulldog

Makes old man grumpy sounds every time he poops or lies down.

BMO

2 YEARS

51.6% Poodle (Small)
25.5% Chihuahua
22.9% Supermutt

Plays with her blueberries before eating them.

Gus

8 YEARS

100.0% American Bully

Shocks his family when they discover he's not part hippopotamus but is, in fact, a purebred dog.

THANK YOU

When I put out the call for help with this project, I received such an outpouring of support that it will never be forgotten! This book was a community effort, and it couldn't have been possible without the cooperation and love of all those involved.

To my incredible photo crew—Glenn Chivens, Adam Hendershott, Tessa Bodey, Genevieve Lee, Dr. Lisa Hsuan, Jules Netley, Roman Cortez, and Olivia Anderson—because of your positivity, kindness, and overall amazing vibes, you made this experience memorable and magical for every dog and person that stepped onto our set. Special thanks to Sarah DeRemer, for all your help with the casting process, and to Lucia Tran and Harley, for helping us test the lighting.

To my editor, Ann Treistman, for believing in this book; to Allison Chi, for helping make this book look beautiful; and to the amazing team at Countryman Press, for all your work behind the scenes bringing this book to life.

To the team at Embark Veterinary—Pamela Leskar, Halli Melnitsky, Mackenzie Pearson, Winette Vo, and others behind the scenes—for your excitement and support of this project. It is a dream to partner with you! Thank you to Dr. David Haworth, for your thoughtful foreword. And my deepest gratitude to the Embark scientists and vets who further research for the well-being of our beloved dogs, and who satiate our curiosity about all these beautiful mystery mutts.

To every single dog and human who participated in this book: It was pure joy to meet you and to photograph your dogs. I loved discovering every unique and charming aspect of your pups. Thank you for being a part of this project.

To the dog rescue and animal shelter community: The majority of the dogs in this book are rescues and wouldn't be here without you. I know how hard and thankless rescue work can be, and I extend my utmost gratitude to you for loving these animals and giving them a second chance at life. To the rescues and shelters that saved the lives of the dogs in this book—Adopt and Shop, Allegheny Abused Animal Relief Fund, Angel City Pitbulls, Barks and Bitches, Big Love Animal Rescue, Bonsall Animal Shelter, Carson Animal Shelter, Champaign County Humane Society, Colorado Puppy Rescue, Deity Animal Rescue and Foundation, Doggie Protective Services Rescue, Family Dog Rescue, Fur Baby Rescue, HIT Living Foundation, Home Free, Humane Society, LA County Animal Shelter, Labelle Foundation, Love Leo Rescue, MaeDay Rescue, Mutt Scouts, Newport Beach Animal Shelter, Ozzie and Friends, Paw Works, Pups Without Borders, Purposeful Rescue, South LA Animal Shelter, Wagmor Pets Dog Rescue, Wags & Walks, West Valley Animal Shelter, Westside German Shepherd Rescue, Wish for Animals—thank you, thank you, thank you.

To my friends and family who supported me behind the scenes during the creation process of this book, I extend my eternal love and appreciation. Your delight as I shared this project with you gave me so much encouragement. A deep bow of gratitude to Mukunda Lal Ghosh and Bonni McCliss for your higher guidance. And to the people to whom I owe the most gratitude—my dear husband, Vincent, and children, Jasper and Elliot—thank you for being my reason for everything. I love you to the moon and back, forever and ever and ever.